What Do
You Mean I Have
Attention
Deficit
Disorder?

What Do You Mean I Have ATTENTION DEFICIT DISORDER?

Kathleen M. Dwyer

Photographs by
Gregg A. Flory

WALKER AND COMPANY

NEW YORK

First published in the United States of America in 1996 by
Walker Publishing Company, Inc.
Published simultaneously in Canada by Thomas Allen & Son Canada, Limited,
Markham, Ontario

Library of Congress Cataloging-in-Publication Data
Dwyer, Kathleen Marshall, 1931–
What do you mean I have attention deficit disorder?/
Kathleen M. Dwyer; photographs by Gregg A. Flory.
p. cm.
Includes bibliographical references and index.
Summary: Follows eleven-year-old Patrick's activities
at home and at school until he is diagnosed with attention-deficit
hyperactivity disorder and learns how to deal with it.
ISBN 0-8027-8392-9 (hardcover). —ISBN 0-8027-8393-7 (reinforced)
1. Attention-deficit hyperactivity disorder—Juvenile literature.
[1. Attention-deficit hyperactivity disorder.]
I. Flory, Gregg M., ill.   II. Title.
RJ506. H9D86 1996
618.92'8589—dc20   95-44556
                                                          CIP
                                                          AC

Book design by Ann Gold

Printed in the United States of America

2 4 6 8 10 9 7 5 3 1

This book is dedicated to
Gregory Francis Dwyer

We would like to thank Patrick and his family,
as well as all the children and teachers
who made this project so enjoyable.

Patrick had been in trouble for as long as he could remember. He didn't try to annoy everyone, but it just seemed to happen. He had often heard his grandmother say to his mom, "Don't worry about Patrick, he will settle down when he gets a little older."

But he was getting older all the time. Just last month he started sixth grade, and he was already eleven years old. It seemed to Patrick that just getting older didn't change anything.

Patrick decided he didn't like school. The teachers were always yelling at him. He got tired of hearing, "Finish your work! Don't you know everyone else has handed in theirs? Now we must wait for Patrick again."

To complicate things, in sixth grade he had to change classes. Now he had more than one teacher telling him, "Pay attention, pay attention." That is all they ever seemed to say! Could Patrick help it if he thought about other things a lot? He kept saying school was boring, but it was really just a place where he was not very happy.

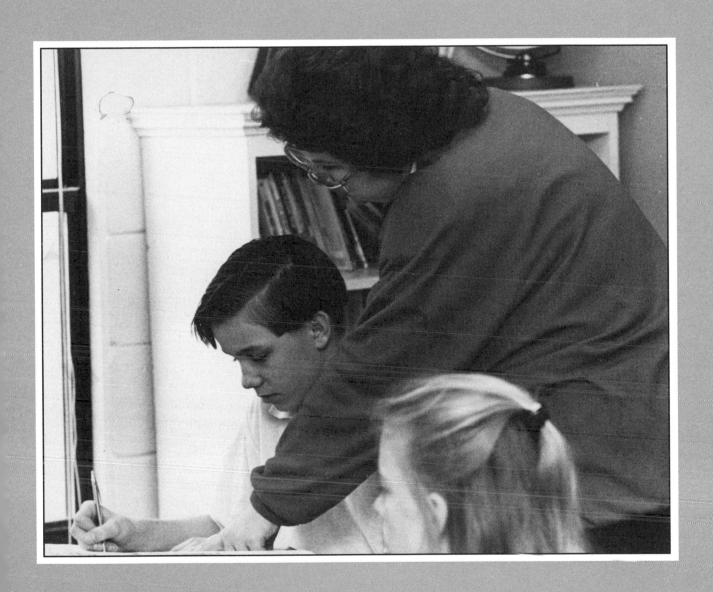

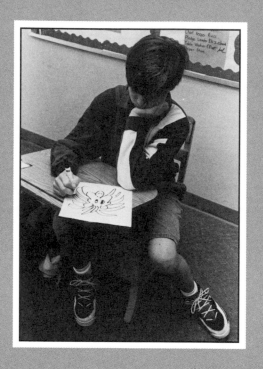

One day in math class, when Mr. Norris was teaching fractions at the board, Patrick began to make animal noises to go with the monster pictures he was drawing. He knew he was being a pest.

Mr. Norris took the drawings away from Patrick and said that he would speak to him after class.

It was so hard for Patrick to follow the instructions when Mr. Norris was showing the class a new kind of problem. Patrick didn't know why he couldn't listen. He prepared for another lecture, just like he'd had a hundred times before.

After all the other kids left the room, Mr. Norris came over to Patrick's desk and said, "Why do you act so silly in school?"

Patrick thought for a long time. "Mr. Norris, I really don't mean to be in trouble so much. It just seems to happen."

Then Patrick started thinking about Terrible Tuesday. His trouble began in social studies class with Mrs. Foley. Patrick thought that the morning would never be over.

He knew that when he was impatient, he either started to play pranks in the classroom or he started thinking of other things. Tuesday was definitely Patrick's day for thinking of other things. When he was supposed to take notes from the board, his thoughts drifted off.

Patrick lived near the ocean and he loved the marsh. He enjoyed watching the birds and the frisky fiddler crabs that scurried across the beach. He loved chasing the seagulls to make them fly.

Patrick ended up just sitting there in school, wondering how all the beautiful creatures of the marsh were doing. He hoped that someday he would be the captain of a shrimp boat like his uncle Greg.

Suddenly Mrs. Foley yelled at him to keep his mind on his vocabulary list.

Then, in health class, the teacher reminded him to stay in his seat. One of the worst things about school was that someone was always telling him to sit still. They wanted him to be like a statue, sitting on those hard chairs all day long. But it wasn't simple to sit still. His legs would start to tingle, and he just had to move them. After that, he just couldn't stay still. Then would come "Sit still, Patrick! Don't you know that you are interrupting the whole class?"

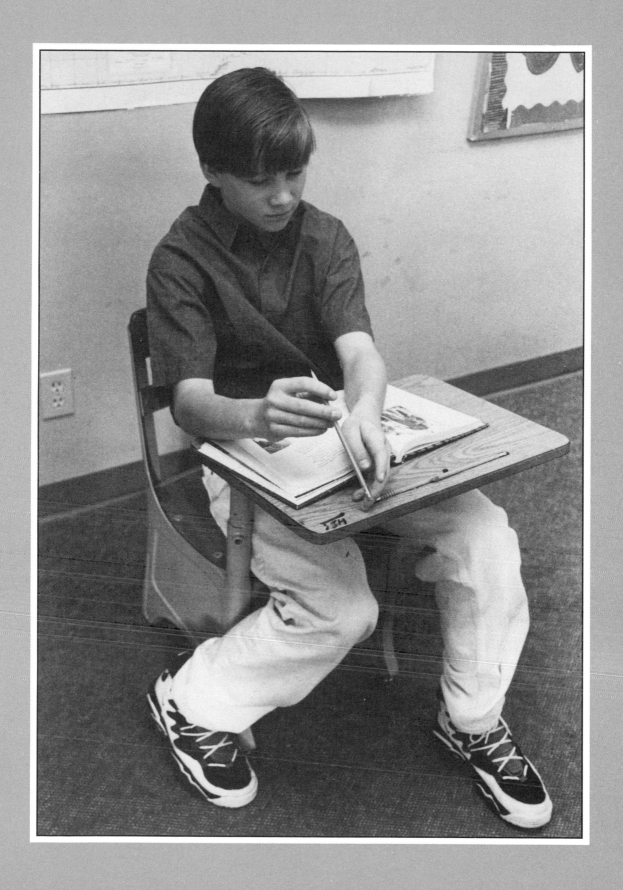

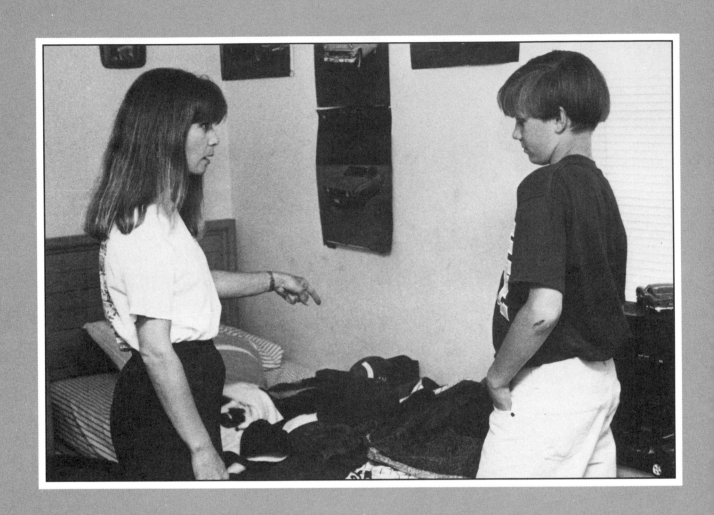

Even at home, his dad called him Little Wiggly Boy.

"I can't help it, Dad," Patrick often replied. Patrick knew that his mom and dad loved him, but he got in trouble at home too. It seemed to Patrick that his mother was always yelling, "What did I just ask you to do? Did you forget already?" Patrick always seemed to forget what he was supposed to do when it was his turn to do a chore.

When he came in from school one day, his mom said, "Patrick, what has been going on in school? Your homeroom teacher, Miss Hogan, called me to set up a special appointment."

"Nothing, Mom, honest, I didn't do anything. She's just picking on me again," said Patrick. But he was really worried about what his parents and Miss Hogan would talk about.

On the day of the meeting, Miss Hogan came right to the point. "I have been observing Patrick since the beginning of this school year. You were wise to request that Patrick be evaluated at the end of last term. The psychologist has finished the testing. It shows that Patrick is a very bright boy. He has an excellent I.Q., but his achievement in math, reading, and written expression is below what we should be seeing from him. He has a considerable problem keeping his mind on his work and following directions."

Mr. and Mrs. Stone agreed with Miss Hogan about Patrick being smart. His dad said, "We see so many ingenious things that he does around home, but several of Patrick's teachers have told us how he has trouble being patient. He can't seem to keep his thoughts organized to do an assignment."

Both parents commented that Patrick was never bored. He had so much energy and curiosity. He was impulsive, and he had a great sense of adventure. It was good to find a teacher who seemed to understand that there was more to their boy than tests could show.

Miss Hogan said, "There is one more thing that you need to do. I think you should take Patrick to his pediatrician to rule out Attention Deficit Disorder."

Patrick's dad was not so sure there was anything wrong with his son. But he agreed that they should find out all they could about why Patrick was having so much trouble.

Mrs. Stone was relieved when they made an appointment with Dr. Lennon, the pediatrician, for the very next day. She was hoping the doctor could help Patrick be happier.

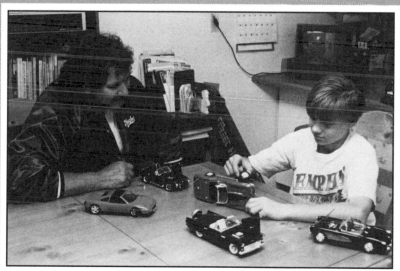

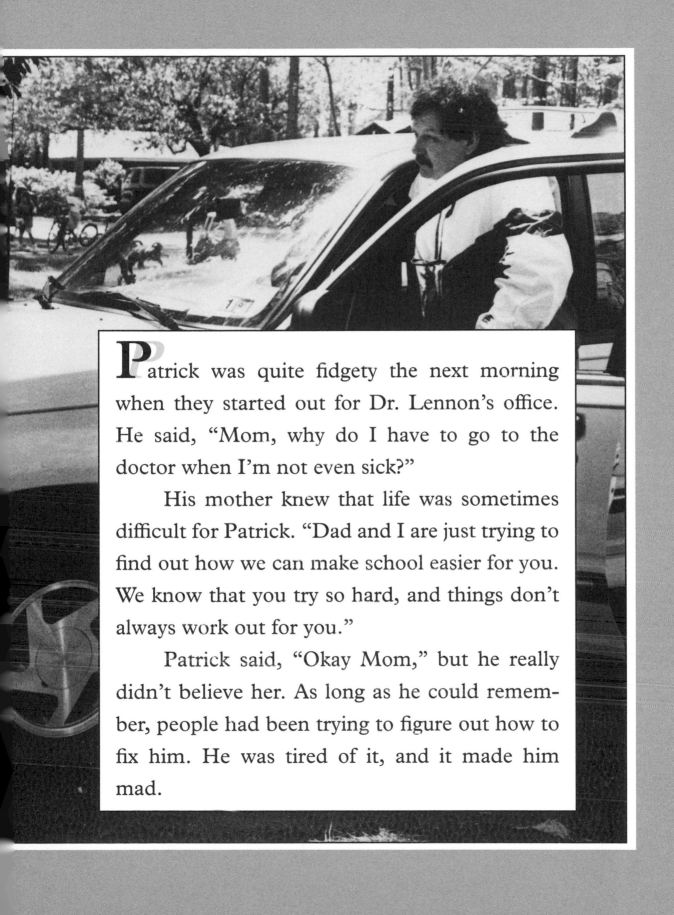

Patrick was quite fidgety the next morning when they started out for Dr. Lennon's office. He said, "Mom, why do I have to go to the doctor when I'm not even sick?"

His mother knew that life was sometimes difficult for Patrick. "Dad and I are just trying to find out how we can make school easier for you. We know that you try so hard, and things don't always work out for you."

Patrick said, "Okay Mom," but he really didn't believe her. As long as he could remember, people had been trying to figure out how to fix him. He was tired of it, and it made him mad.

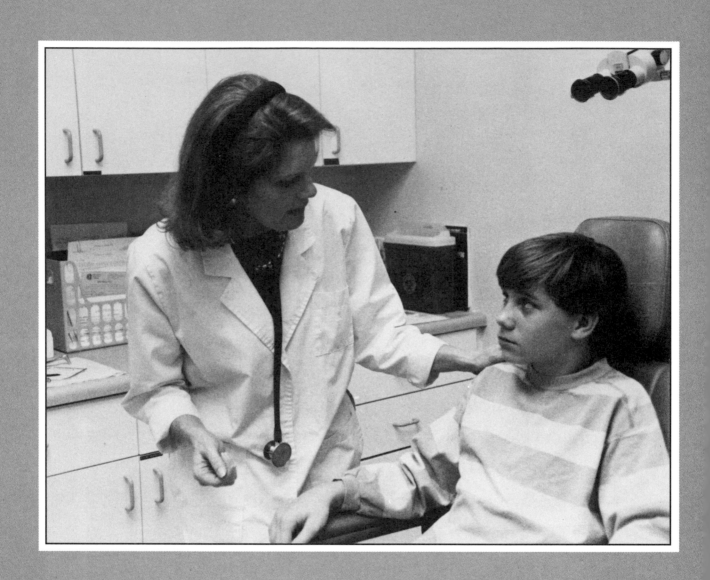

After Dr. Lennon checked Patrick over, she started asking Mrs. Stone some questions. She reminded Patrick's mother that there were many comments in his records about how hard it was for Patrick in school. Mrs. Stone explained that Patrick had a new homeroom teacher this year who believed that Patrick was smart, although he had difficulty getting through the school day.

"There is a very common behavior disorder that is really a medical condition. It affects concentration, impulse control, and attention. It is called Attention Deficit Disorder. Patrick has several symptoms that together paint a picture for us," remarked Dr. Lennon. "It includes inattention, impulsivity, and often, overactive behavior. You know how everyone describes Patrick as that boy who can't sit still."

"That's true, Doctor," replied Mrs. Stone. "Our Patrick does seem to move all the time." Patrick's mother smiled down at Patrick as he moved closer to her. "Do you really think that is the explanation for Patrick's problem?"

"We will carefully rule out all other medical conditions, but I believe that Patrick has Attention Deficit Disorder, or A.D.D. for short," said Dr. Lennon.

"What do you mean I have A.D.D?" asked Patrick.

"Patrick, all the folks who care about you seem to notice that it is hard for you to concentrate and that you get distracted easily. We notice that you have great energy. That is very good for being curious about many things. Having speedy energy isn't good, though, when you rush to do something before you think about what will happen. You can be doing one job and before you know it, you have your mind on something else. Isn't that right, Patrick?" said Dr. Lennon. "Attention means thinking hard about something. Deficit means you lack it. So all it means is that you do not have good attention when you are thinking about doing a particular job. Does that make sense, Patrick?"

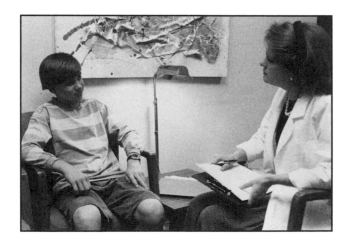

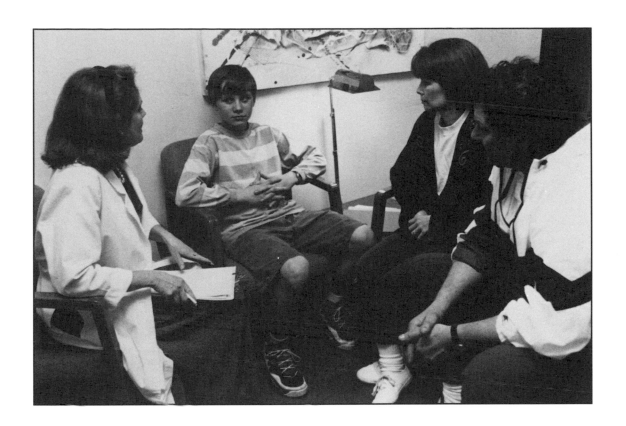

"Yeah, Doctor. Teachers are always telling me that I don't pay attention," said Patrick. Dr. Lennon explained that the good news was that you could be very smart and still have this condition.

"Are you sure that I'm not just dumb?" said Patrick.

"Actually, I'd say that you are just too smart. Your mind thinks of too many things at the same time," said Dr. Lennon.

Dr. Lennon then turned to Patrick's parents and explained that treatment works best with educational management. A.D.D is not something that you treat only with medication. Some children do need medication, but it usually lasts for only a short time.

Patrick needed to learn how to gain more control over his restless energy. This would take considerable effort by his teachers, parents, and Patrick himself.

Dr. Lennon said that Patrick may need a combination of treatments, including medication, but the first step should be at school, because that is where life is hardest for him. "I have heard good things about the school's approach with children like Patrick," added Dr. Lennon.

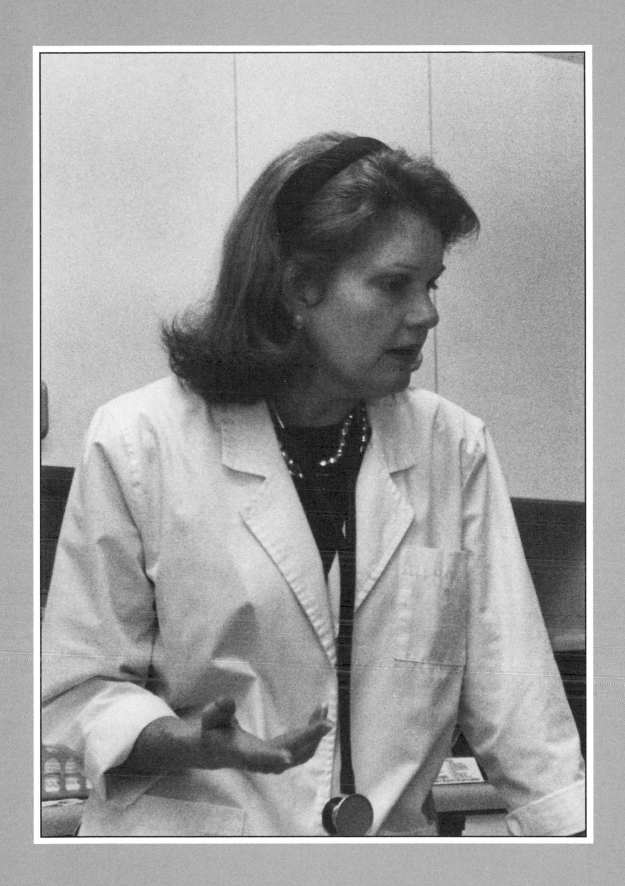

Because of Patrick's high energy level, sports are very good activities. Patrick's mom said, "He enjoys playing sports very much." Dr. Lennon agreed that sports would help Patrick use some of his exceptional energy.

Mrs. Stone paused for a minute and wondered if Patrick's problem was their fault, because they both got impatient when he had difficulty following directions around the house. Dr. Lennon replied, "No, raising children with A.D.D. just requires a lot of stamina. There are several good support groups that might help you by sharing some experiences about other A.D.D. children. And Patrick might enjoy meeting and talking to other kids who have the same problems he has."

A few weeks later Patrick's mother received a phone call from Miss Hogan. She told Mrs. Stone that the teachers had put many procedures to work to make Patrick's school day better. Miss Hogan asked Mr. and Mrs. Stone to come to a meeting so that the teachers, Patrick, and his parents could all know the rules.

The following day after school, Patrick's mother and father went to meet his teachers. They felt good that so many people were trying to help Patrick find a way to do well in school. Most of his usual teachers were there, and Patrick had been asked to come to the meeting, too. He was a bit nervous, because whenever there was a meeting with teachers, it usually meant bad news for him.

Miss Hogan thanked everyone for coming and explained that they all wanted to help Patrick find a way to do better in school. The teachers talked about some things they did in school that could also help at home. Miss Hogan said that nice soft music helped Patrick settle down as he came into class in the morning. A "Take Home" checklist taped to his cubby helps Patrick remember his homework. Now he could no longer use the excuse that he forgot his books. "Even the bus driver asks me if I have forgotten my backpack if he sees me trying to get on the bus without my books. I can't get away with anything anymore," said Patrick with a smile.

Another reminder that was very helpful was a system of colored folders for keeping track of different subjects.

"**D**ad," said Patrick, "it is really cool. All my language books have a red cover or a red number one on them. The math book and my math notes have a green cover and number two. Social studies is yellow and number three. Science is blue and number four. It helps me to find things. Lots of times I knew that I did an assignment but the teacher yelled at me because I couldn't find it."

The Blue Book Method

AN ASSOC...
KEY WORD...

STUDENT
REFERENCE
SHEETS
AND
WRITING
EXERCISES
For Independent Work

Crayola

THE BLUE BOOK Pg. 34
STUDENT REFERENCE SHEET Pg.14

The Spellings of \ō
6 ways to spell \ō\ sound

• DIVIDE each word into Syllables and UNDERLINE Spelling Component for the KEY WORD SOUND.

o - pony	o-e - home	oa - boat
po-lite	broke	loaf-er
fro-mus	close	float
I-da-ho	spoke	throat
cro-cus	toe	load

The Spellings of \ō
6 ways to spell \ō\ sound

• DIVIDE each word into Syllables and UNDERLINE Spelling Component for the KEY WORD SOUND.

THE BLUE BOOK Pg. 34
STUDENT REFERENCE SHEET Pg.14

oe - toe	ough - though	ow - snow
goes	al-though	yel-low
doe	dough	flow
ech-oes	bor-ough	mel-low
he-roes		grown

To remind Patrick to wait his turn before he interrupts the social studies class, Mrs. Foley has pasted a small cutout hand to his desk. When Patrick sees it, he is reminded to raise his hand.

"I don't always remember, but most of the time it does help me keep out of trouble," said Patrick.

Patrick was starting to feel good about being at this conference. He had been having a better time in school, and it even sounded like he might be doing something right for a change.

The language arts teacher mentioned Patrick's listening difficulties, which sometimes cause him to mix up words and the sounds of letters. "His spelling and reading are being improved by a system of associative keywords for sounds. Patrick is remembering his spelling rules so much better."

Miss Hogan added, "His resource teacher is using perceptual techniques to correct his visual-spatial problems. She also works on his weak memory so he will be able to remember what he has read or heard."

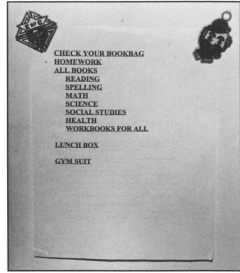

CHECK YOUR BOOKBAG
HOMEWORK
ALL BOOKS
    READING
    SPELLING
    MATH
    SCIENCE
    SOCIAL STUDIES
    HEALTH
    WORKBOOKS FOR ALL

LUNCH BOX

GYM SUIT

Math is not one of Patrick's favorite subjects, and he often feels restless. A work station at the side of the room lets Patrick stand while working with his math rods. "They do a great deal of mental math, and Patrick thinks fast on his feet," explained Miss Hogan. "Graph paper helps him to keep his numbers straight."

Several teachers suggested ways to help Patrick at home. He doesn't seem to notice how much time is passing. To help him estimate how long chores and homework take, the teachers suggested he time them. He could use an egg timer for short jobs, a cooking timer for longer ones. Patrick can race against the timer. Another way to help would be to set aside specific times for his various jobs.

The teachers pointed out that Patrick needed to be reminded a bit more than other children, but long lectures don't help. A checklist of jobs he is expected to do around home is helpful.

Patrick spoke up. "I like that one you put at the door for my 'Take to School' list."

Mrs. Stone confided that these problems run in her family. Patrick is proud to say that his uncle Jim, who has A.D.D. too, is now a successful salesman.

Mr. and Mrs. Stone were happy as they left the meeting. Mr. Stone said, "Thank you so much for all the thoughtful care you have given Patrick. We appreciate it very much and know that Patrick will do very well one day, and we are very proud of him."

As time went on Mrs. Stone noticed that Patrick was doing better in school and at home. Because he now stopped and thought before racing into something, his mom knew that he was developing an inner voice that helped him to talk things over with himself. He was taking the time to read instructions before answering questions. He made sure the trash bags were tied before he took them out to the garbage cans. It did seem that knowing the routines at school and at home was helpful. Patrick knows that he is as smart as anyone else.

SOURCES OF HELP

**The American Academy
of Audiology**
1735 North Lynn Street
Suite 950
Arlington, VA 22209-2022

**American Psychological
Association**
750 First Street N.E.
Washington, D.C. 20002
(202) 336-5500

**Children and Adults with
Attention Deficit Disorder
(CHADD)**
499 Northwest 70th Avenue,
Suite 101
Plantation, FL 33317
(800) 233-4050
(305) 587-3700

**National ADD Association
Support Network Information
Line**
(800) 487-2282

**National Institute of Child
Health and Human
Development**
National Institutes of Health
U.S. Department of Health and
Human Services
Building 31
Bethesda, MD 20205
(301) 496-5133

**National Institute for Learning
Disabilities**
107 Seekel Street
Norfolk, VA 23505
(804) 423-8646

The Orton Dyslexia Society
Chester Building
8600 La Salle Road
Baltimore, MD 21286-2044